Inspired Flower Arrangements

Inspired Flower Arrangements
Toshiro Kawase

Foreword by Issey Miyake

Kodansha International
Tokyo · New York · London

The publisher would like to thank the following publishers, temples, shrines, institutions, and persons who granted permission to reproduce photographs or objects in their collections:

Hōnen'in Temple, Hatakeyama Museum, Daichūji Temple, Gotō Art Museum, Daihōin Temple, Nishi-Honganji Temple, Kōzanji Temple, Rokuōin Temple, Nagoya Railroad Co., Ltd., Myōki-an, Tokyo National Museum, Yōmei-bunko, Imperial Household Agency, Kōzō Okada, Masako Shirasu.

Plate numbers 1, 15, 21–22, 58–60, 62 are from *Hana wa No ni Aruyōni*, published in 1984 by
　Tankōsha Publishing Co., Ltd.
12–14, 25, 45–46, 55, 63 are from *Hana to Utsuwa*, published in 1983 by Kannashobō Publishing Co., Ltd.
26–27, 48–51, 53, 62 are from *Kateigahō*, published by Sekaibunka-sha.
28, 36–41 are from *Taiyō*, published in 1988 by Heibonsha Ltd.
2–3, 20, 47, 54, 57, 74 are from *Fūshikaden*, published in 1981 by Bunka Publishing Bureau.
4–11, 16–17, 23–24, 29–35, 42–44, 64, 66–73 are by Kodansha Planning Editorial Center Ltd.
52, 56 are from *Sophia*, published in 1985 by Kodansha Ltd.

Book design by **Kōichi Satō**.
Translation by **Juliet Winters Carpenter**.
Photographs by **Tsunehiro Kobayashi**: plate numbers 1–3, 12–15, 18–22, 25–27, 45–63, 65, 74.
Tadashi Ōmori: plate numbers 4–11, 16–17, 23–24, 28–44, 64, 66–70, 72–73.
Shirō Senba: plate number 71.

Previously published in a larger format under the same title, *Inspired Flower Arrangements*.

Distributed in the United States by Kodansha America, Inc., 114 Fifth Avenue, New York, N.Y., 10011, and in the United Kingdom and continental Europe by Kodansha Europe Ltd., 95 Aldwych, London WC2B 4JF. Published by Kodansha International Ltd., 17–14, Otowa 1-chome, Bunkyo-ku, Tokyo 112–8652, and Kodansha America, Inc.

Library of Congress Cataloging in Publication Data available.

ISBN 4-7700-2386-3
First edition, 1990
New hardcover edition, 1999
99 00 01 02 03　5 4 3 2 1

Contents

Foreword

As an occasional visitor to flower arrangement exhibitions, I cannot recall ever once having been deeply moved. Panoplies of works by artists of competing schools rise before me through a vague mist, like apparitions from some other world.

I do remember clearly, however, that my conception of the art was transformed by my first encounter with the *tatehana* ("standing flower") pieces of Toshirō Kawase. In fact I was amazed by what I can only call his magical powers.

He is like a master swordsman pulling off impossible feats, or a Magus conjuring all manner of things out of empty space, or an ancient writer of love poems. His mysterious ceremony unfolds in beauty, amid grand, flowing natural rhythms that echo in the soul. I was profoundly moved by his every gesture, by the subtleties of his use of emptiness, and by the depth of his insight into the life of flowers. Slowly he identifies with the flowers until, in some incredibly sensuous way, he is one with them. I was reminded of Nō dancing, out of which arose the medieval aesthetic of *hana* ("flower"): a sense of freshness and compelling realism, accompanied by deep emotion and a startled awareness that one is seeing something familiar for the first time.

As one who responds best to the beauty of flowers growing wild in their natural environments, I believe we all have the right to appreciate flowers individually, each in our own way. What makes Mr. Kawase's *tatehana* arrangements so moving is their vivid manifestation of the dual principles of motion and stillness as they interact in nature.

I find the world of Toshirō Kawase—where, with complete naturalness and consummate skill, a flower's momentary spark is transformed into an act of artistic creation—at once enviable, and vaguely unsettling.

Issey Miyake

1

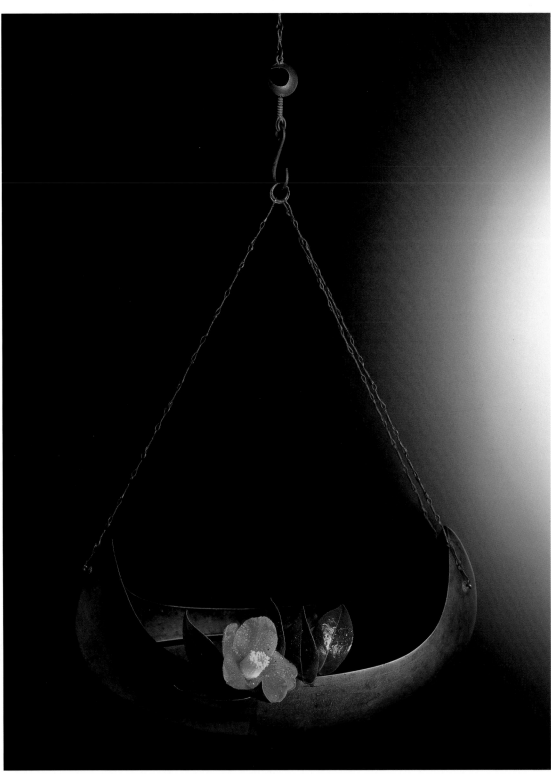

2

4

12-a

12-b

12-c

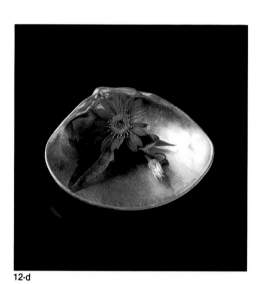

12-d

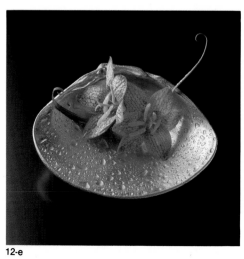

12-e

12-f

13

14

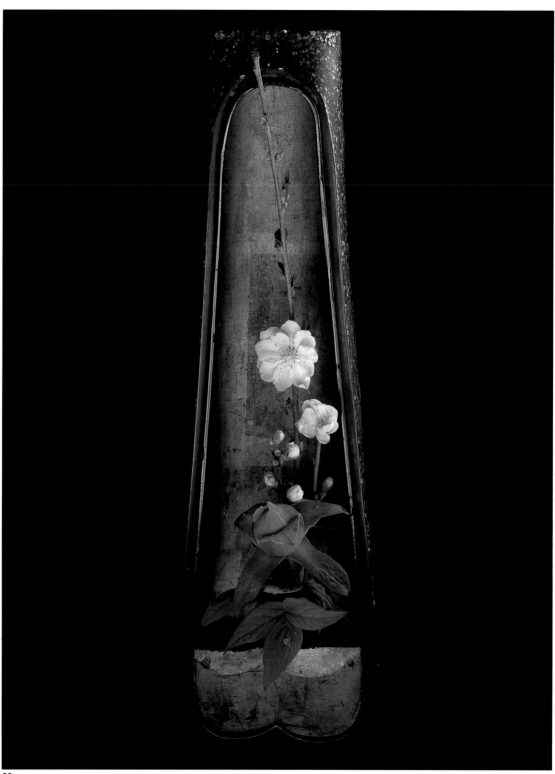

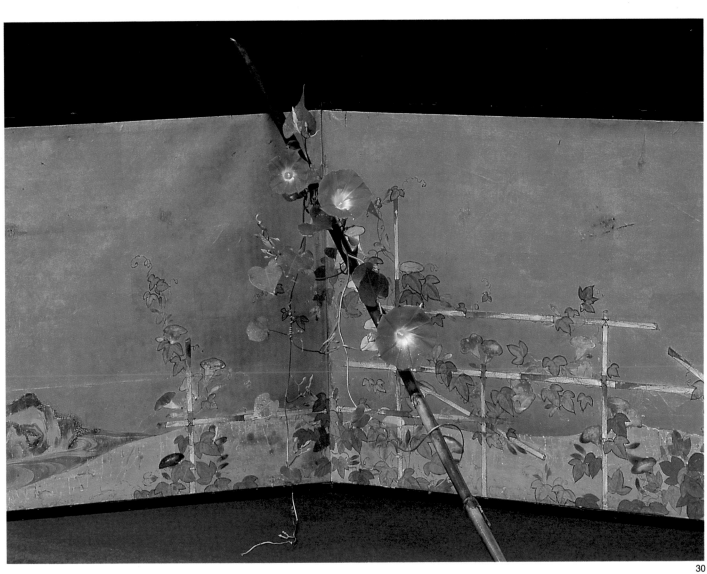

36

37

42-a

49

50

52

67-a

67-b

67-c

67-d

67-e

67-f

The Universe in a Single Flower

Throughout human history, in East and West alike, the beauty of flowers has added grace and charm to people's lives. Why, then, has the art of *ikebana*—flower arrangement, as distinct from flower design—arisen only in Japan? To answer that question, I would like to consider the historical background of ikebana, and trace the development of its spirit, which culminates in the view that the whole universe is contained within a single flower.

"Standing Flowers" and the Concept of *Yorishiro*
In Japan, where the great natural beauty of the country is enhanced by rich seasonal variation, people have long been drawn to plants and flowers.

The *Nihon Shoki* (*Chronicles of Japan*, A.D. 720), Japan's oldest official history, contains the statement that "all plants can speak"—thus attributing human qualities to natural objects. Out of this sense of intimacy with nature, and wonder at the blooming and scattering of flowers, ancient Japanese gave their gods names like Kono-hana-saku-ya-hime (Princess Flowering Trees) and Kono-hana-chiru-hime (Princess Scattering Blossoms).

Ancient Japanese saw elements of the divine everywhere in nature; an animistic polytheism arose in Japan (totally at variance with the monotheistic tradition of the West) that saw gods in every stone, tree, and flower, as well as in the wind and earth. Japanese gods were in fact nomads. The Shinto shrines we see today came about only after the introduction of Buddhism exposed people to the magnificence of temple architecture. And so, rather than making pilgrimages to holy places, Japanese people summoned their vagrant gods to come to them as the need arose. A special ceremony or festival known as *kami-mukae* (god-welcoming) was held to celebrate the gods' arrival. As landmarks to guide the gods on their way, or as antennae to "catch" them, people used plants. Flowers, being short-lived, were passed over in favor of long-lasting evergreens; these, deemed fit shelter for the gods, were set up as tall and straight as possible to wel-

Pine trees arranged in the *yorishiro* style. Arrangement by the author. Photograph by Tsunehiro Kobayashi.

come them. They became known as *yorishiro*—places for the gods to enter.

Japanese flower arranging thus originated with this sacred act of welcoming a god or gods. The sacredness of the act constituted the essence of ikebana, and is the source from which the world of ikebana developed into the form we know today.

Even now, during the New Year's holidays, Japanese people put up pine trees at their gates to welcome the god of the new year. This, too, is a form of *yorishiro*, as is the pine tree painted symbolically on the back of a Nō stage: the play is performed for the benefit of the god within the pine.

Kuge—Buddhist Ritual Flower Offerings

The sense of sacredness at the core of ikebana derives not only from Shinto tradition but from Buddhism as well. The Buddhist religion was transmitted to Japan from China in the sixth century, a period when Chinese culture had an almost overwhelming impact here, shaking the Japanese way of thinking to its very foundations. Because of Shinto's polytheism, with its belief in *yaoyorozu no kami*, or gods virtually without number, Japan was able to accept the very different religion of Buddhism in a general spirit of toleration, without anything approaching religious conflict, and assimilate it readily into existing patterns of belief.

Shinto gods may have been formless and homeless, except when summoned on occasion to enter a *yorishiro*, but the new religion had tangible Buddhist images set in special sacred places—the temple sanctuaries. Buddhist monks accordingly had to conduct religious services daily, the year round.

The significance of Buddhism in the development of ikebana lies in ritual flower offerings called *kuge*. The custom of solemnly placing flowers before a Buddhist image, an important part of memorial services for the dead, originated in India—as did *sange*, the ritual of scattering petals, which began as a way of welcoming people or seeing them off, and *keman*, ritual implements in the shape of stylized floral wreaths, which can be traced back to the custom of adorning the body with wreaths. In all of these, it is notable that only the petals or crown of the flower are used. As Buddhism spread to China, it became more common to place flowers in vases—usually lotus blossoms or the like, in vases with narrow necks.

At first, Japanese adherents of Buddhism merely followed the Chinese example, but in the Heian period (A.D. 794–1185), as the Buddhist faith took root in the lives of individuals, and Japan made the transition from direct imitation of Chinese culture to the development of its own culture, flower offerings gradually became Japanized. Gradually, the old Shinto concept of *yorishiro* was transplanted to the Buddhist environment, so that the flower offerings took on sacred aspects in themselves. At the same time, emphasis shifted from the color and perfume of the petals alone to the entire flower—stem, leaves, and all—as a symbol of the unity of heaven and earth.

The Tale of Genji, the great Heian classic of Japanese literature, contains a description of hanging a mandala and "arranging flowers high in a silver vase." As this passage makes clear, flowers were placed straight up in vases. Such standing flower offerings (*tateru kuge*), a mixture of ancient Shinto and Buddhist traditions, developed into *tatehana* ("standing flowers"), an early prototype of modern ikebana.

The Nō stage at Nishi Honganji Temple, Kyoto. A stylized pine tree is painted on the back wall.

In this reproduction from the Scrolls of *Frolicking Animals* and *Humans* (*Chōjū giga*, twelfth century), a monkey dressed as a Buddhist priest recites sutras to a frog Buddha; between them is a *kuge*.

The Influence of Buddhist Architecture

Temple architecture was another important Buddhist influence on the development of ikebana. In Japan, as we have seen, nature itself was considered divine, so that Shinto gods needed no protection from the elements. *Yorishiro*, their temporary abodes, were generally set up outdoors, and removed as soon as the ceremony or occasion was over. Buddhism, in contrast, had temples on fixed sites, and flower offerings were naturally made indoors. The spread of Buddhism in Japan also signified a shift in focus from an outdoor lifestyle to an indoor one.

Heian Japanese developed a native architectural style known as *shinden-zukuri* (the "palace style"); soon it became customary to plant gardens in the forecourt and middle court. At the same time, plant life was brought indoors in the form of a type of tray landscape called *suhama*, or "sandy beach"; in this way natural plants were beginning to be represented in a stylized, symbolic fashion, losing their religious connotations little by little and becoming purely decorative.

From Decoration to Amusement

The first flower offerings were made with evergreens, and Buddhist influence made the lotus popular; gradually, though, the increasing use of seasonal flowers heightened interest in a wide variety of plants.

From there it was a short step to plucking a spray of cherry blossoms and arranging it in a vase as decoration: Another Heian literary masterpiece, the *Pillow Book* of Sei Shōnagon (*c.* 1000), has a passage describing the pleasure its author took in doing just that: "I placed a large blue vase by the railing, and filled it with a long spray of really exquisite cherry blossoms—so many that they hung down over the railing." The spray was, she indicates, about a meter and a half long. Contemporary literature contains many such descriptions of flowers used to decorate rooms where guests were to be entertained.

As the custom of arranging flowers indoors for pleasure became increasingly popular, interest also arose in accompanying details, such as the best type of container to use and the best place to put an arrangement. At the same time, flowers were adopted more and more frequently as motifs in poetry, literature, and painting; people's interest in and observation of flowers deepened, sharpening their sense of the seasons as well as their ability to judge floral beauty.

Heian aristocrats did not stop there, but also used flowers in a lively indoor game. "Flower-matching" (*hana-awase*) became a popular, elegant pastime, along with many other games involving the comparison of various objects (*mono-awase*). In all such games, contestants would form two teams, Right and Left, and line up opposite each other, each with an item brought for judgment. Unless otherwise specified, the flower was cherry blossoms, but all sorts of contests were held with other flowers as well, throughout the year. In this way people came to share an understanding and appreciation of the four seasons, with a common vocabulary and a common love of seasonal hues and variations.

Hana-awase arrangement by the author. Photograph by Tsunehiro Kobayashi.

Miyabi and the Double Structure of the Japanese Aesthetic Sense

The Heian aesthetic ideal of *miyabi*, or elegance, arose out of just such elegant leisure activities as those described above. The word *miyabi* derives from *miya*, the Japanese word for palace, and denotes a refined elegance and brilliance. At the same time, however, it embraces contrasting notions of transience, mutability, and evanescence.

Looking happily on a gorgeous scene of cherry blossoms in full bloom, the viewer would be filled at the same time by a sense of impending loss, knowing the blossoms were destined soon to fall. Sadness and delight would be registered side by side within the viewer's heart.

This duality, or tendency to be aware of a constant tension and balance between opposites—ornate beauty and quiet simplicity, motion and stillness, life and death—is a distinguishing feature of Japanese culture.

Matsuo Bashō (1644–94), the great haiku master, used the word *zōka* for nature. The first character of the compound means to make or create, and the second to change shape. This reflects a view of nature as something not fixed and permanent but ever-changing—a view which corresponds with the traditional Japanese view of nature. (Such a view is certainly not uniquely Japanese; it resembles that of ancient Greece, where "Nature" was taken as the power to animate and to create.)

One more important element in the philosophical view of nature leading to Japan's double aesthetic was the sense that nature was not an object to contend with or to conquer, but something to live in and with. The Japanese believe that all living things share the capacity to feel and that, like humans, they are only temporary manifestations of life, subject to transmigration and sharing ultimately in the common fate of all.

The Japanese empathy with the life and death of flowers is reflected inevitably in the very word "ikebana," which is derived from *ikeru* (living, to keep alive) and *hana* (flowers).

The dual nature of the Japanese aesthetic sense arises from the attempt to see beyond the flower before one's eyes to the hidden, inner "heart" of the flower—just as people in love seek to know and possess each other's true hearts.

All Japanese art, not only ikebana, springs inevitably from this view of nature. Using material phenomena to express incorporeal spirit has been the traditional concern of Japanese art, and accordingly the chief goal of the Japanese artist has been to grasp the inner heart of his subject.

In ikebana, because the goal is not to grasp the flower itself but the soul of all living plants, the principal flowers used are wildflowers that have braved the elements and speak in the rugged accents of nature itself. Western flower arranging, on the other hand, has pursued the flower itself, so that flower gardens are highly refined, and Western styles of flower arrangement have made an art out of the flower's natural beauty; garden flowers, not wildflowers, are the principal flowers used.

Architecture and Ikebana—The Advent of the *Tokonoma*

To create ikebana, flowers must be cut, brought indoors, placed in vases filled with life-giving water, and arranged in some pleasing way. The exact form that an arrangement takes will depend on where it is to be put and for what purpose. Thus the form of ikebana has been largely determined by the purposes and spirit of Japanese architecture.

Separated from their religious origins, sacred *tateru kuge* (standing flower offerings) became decorative *tatehana* (standing flowers), rising to a peak of prominence in the Muromachi period (1333–1573). This is when the traditional Japanese style of living became established, and the *shoin-zukuri* type of residential architecture was

Early example of a *tokonoma* (1483 illustration from *Bokie-kotoba*).

Before the development of the *tokonoma*, flowers were used as part of a formal sacred offering before wall scroll. This illustration by the celebrated Muromachi-period flower arranger Mon'ami (d. 1517) depicts the *mitsugusoku*, or three sacred elements—a flower vase, incense, and a candle—on a tray before the scroll, which always displayed a Buddhist theme.

Jo-an of Uraku-en, Aichi (built about 1618). Guests must stoop to enter through the miniature doorway of this *sōan*-style teahouse.

perfected—a style which forms the basis of today's traditional Japanese house. (*Shoin* refers to the library of a Zen monastery.) The most important innovation of this style of architecture for ikebana was the *tokonoma*, an alcove for the display of scrolls, flowers, etc.

Ever since its introduction to Japan in the sixth century, the custom of making flower offerings has undergone a process of Japanization, so that by the Heian period it was being carried out in special rooms in the homes of aristocrats, called *butsuma* (family Buddhist altar-rooms). The *tokonoma*, descending from this sacred ancestor, has evolved into a solemn, sacred space without parallel in Japanese culture: a sacred microcosm. The appearance of this space within which the true meaning of flowers can be expressed—the embodiment of the spirit of Japan—made possible the flourishing of ikebana as we know it.

Nageire

The dual nature of the Japanese aesthetic sense can be seen in architecture as well as ikebana. On the one hand we have the emergence of *shoin-zukuri*, a highly public, standardized form of architecture used for large, magnificent reception areas; in reaction to this opulence emerged simple, natural-seeming structures in a style called *sōan* (also known as *sukiya*), characterized by a rough, primitive appearance.

Sōan is written with the character for "grass," suggesting a hermitage made of woven grass. When the occupant is gone, the grasses will come undone, and the place will revert to its former wild state; it is nothing but a temporary abode. The word *suki*, although written now in different characters, means to be fond of, to have a deep and abiding attachment to something. During the Muromachi period, the *sukiya* became closely associated with the tea ceremony and with the simple, unpretentious spirit of Zen.

The style of flower arrangement associated with these surroundings is free and spontaneous: one or two wildflowers of which the arranger is particularly fond, in a container similarly matching that person's particular taste. Where *tatehana* was highly public, formal, and profound, expressing the sublimity of all Nature, *nageire* (to throw or fling) style arrangements are private, informal, and light, expressing the sublimity of the individual's own universe.

With the sacredness of the *tatehana* style as warp, and the freedom of the *nageire* style as woof, ikebana went on weaving spectacular dramas of the natural world.

Tatehana and Nageire

Having established the importance of these two highly contrasting styles of flower arrangement in the development of ikebana, I should like to turn to some questions of detail: Exactly what sort of flowers did each style use, in what sort of containers, and how?

Because the *tatehana* style still retains strong vestiges of its sacred origins, it begins with the establishment of the central branch, the *shin* (spiritual center)—the branch corresponding most closely to the ancient *yorishiro*. In order to secure the arrangement, this branch must be propped up somehow. Many devices have been tried over the ages, but in *tatehana*, the most common has been something called a *komiwara*: a bundle of straw cores cut to the size of the container. (The spiked *kenzan* commonly used today is simply a metallic version of the upper half of the traditional *komiwara*.)

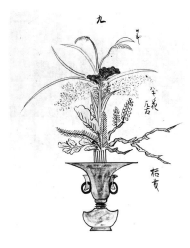

This *tatehana*-style arrangement by Ikenobō Sen'ei (1528–79) is reproduced from a classic work on ikebana, *Ikenobō Sen'ei Sōdensho*.

The *komiwara* is made to fit snugly into the mouth of the vase and almost reach the lip. (In this example, the inside of the vase is only half the vase's actual height). All floral materials must be sharpened so that they can be inserted firmly into the *komiwara*. The *komiwara*'s top is at left; the *kenzan* is at right.

These are the most popular supports for a cylindrical vase. Use branches or stems from available floral materials. The prop is cut as with a pencil sharpener and slightly leveled off at the top. One single stick or two crossed sticks are placed a half-inch below the mouth of the container.

This method employs only branches. A branch is bent so as to press against the sides of the vase. This can be combined with cross supports.

A widely used method of support is the inserting of a separate piece into a split branch.

In contrast, *nageire* arrangements consist almost literally of "throwing" the flower into its container with studied casualness, so that the flower is not anchored at all, but free, relaxed, liberated from all artificial constraints. The only way to secure it is by bending the branch slightly or placing another branch sideways across the mouth of the vase for support.

Containers for *tatehana*, too, tend to be metal Buddhist implements, due to the association with flower offerings. In contrast, *nageire* allows the arranger to use his or her own judgment, choosing from items like porcelain dishes, bamboo vases, baskets, and the like. The *nageire* tradition sees less beauty in using ready-made flower containers and more in finding everyday objects originally made for some other purpose.

The forms of the styles, too, are vastly different. *Tatehana*, after establishing the *shin*, seeks to achieve a perfect balance, following rules like "right long, left short" to achieve symmetry and perfection. *Nageire*, on the other hand, because of the influence of Zen and the austere Way of Tea, deliberately avoids all appearance of symmetry. In the Zen tradition, symmetry is not perfection, but useless, dead repetition.

The two styles do not even use the same type of flower. *Tatehana* centers the composition around an evergreen tree, surrounding it with a profusion of seasonal flowers, as if to include everything from a mountaintop to the foothills in one vase—a colorful floral symphony with which to express the ever-changing beauties of nature.

In contrast, *nageire*, the style suited to the expression of the individual's own inner universe, prefers to draw out small, hidden flowers of the sort that *tatehana* could pass over without a second glance, and give them their share of the limelight. Further, while *tatehana* deliberately chooses flowers and plants that suggest eternity, *nageire* suggests rather flowers that fade quickly, like morning glories, to invest the arrangement with a sense of the momentariness of life.

The Universe in a Single Flower: Hideyoshi and Rikyū

In the Momoyama period (1573–1615), the *shoin-zukuri* style of architecture became progressively more luxurious, elaborate, showy, and rich; similarly, the *tatehana* style of flower arrangement became ever larger, bolder, and brighter.

By contrast, the rustic *soan*-style teahouse became ever smaller and more simplified, as Sen no Rikyū (1522–91) developed his aesthetic ideals and imposed his vision on the tea ceremony. Gradually, the *nageire* style of flower arrangement came to symbolize his aesthetics of simple restraint, so condensed and crystallized that a single flower could represent the life of all nature, and indeed the universe.

The Momoyama period was an age when this aesthetic of *wabi*, or quiet, simple beauty, clashed head-on with the gaudy taste of one of the most famous of Japan's rulers and Rikyū's patron, Toyotomi Hideyoshi (1536–98). The drama of the struggle between the two men, who represented opposite poles of beauty, ended tragically when Rikyū was ordered by Hideyoshi to commit ritual suicide.

What seem to be such different concepts of beauty, however, are in fact twins, born of the Japanese dual conception of Nature and Life. The lonely tranquility of Rikyū's *wabi* was in fact an essential underpinning of the

Tatehana-style arrangement by the author. (See Plate 68.)

Nageire-style arrangement by the author. (See Plate 33.)

Reception Hall of Nishi-Honganji Temple, Kyoto. This ornate example of *shoin-zukuri* was built by Toyotomi Hideyoshi, ruler of Japan in the Momoyama period and known for his love of luxury and power.

The interior of the Tai-an teahouse of Myōkian, Kyoto, represents the austere simplicity of the *soan*-style teahouse. This teahouse was designed by the great tea master Sen no Rikyū.

Nageire-style arrangement by Sen no Rikyū: a camellia in a bamboo vase. From *Sūkibunsho*.

Cherry blossom in a "standing flower"–style arrangement, by Ikenobō Senkō. From *Rikkazu-byōbu*.

showiness (*hana*) of the *shoin* style.

The Momoyama period, thanks to the appearance of the two geniuses Rikyū and Hideyoshi, brought the steady tension between these two opposing, seemingly irreconcilable strands in the Japanese aesthetic tradition to a dramatic climax; through this conflict, each man managed to bring the tradition he represented to unprecedented heights.

In fact, Rikyū's ascetic taste was not irreconcilable with the gay finery of the *hana* style; rather, it was a refinement of it and a reduction to essentials. The words *wabi* and *hana* could be replaced with "natural" and "artificial," which also may seem unalterably opposed, but in fact are not. In Japan, the height of artificiality is naturalness, and the height of naturalness, artificiality.

Japanese art may appear natural, because its origins are in nature. But it has never simply imitated nature. We tend to assume that nature is something obvious and apparent to anyone, but actually, when we seek a true expression of nature, we find it is always changing and impossible to capture. The only way to catch hold of nature is to seize some point of it—the rib of a fan, for example—and make that hardly noticed detail a personal expression of nature.

The teahouses of Sen no Rikyū became steadily more constricted as he refined and compressed his vision, until finally there was barely room for one person to enter. At that point the building ceased altogether to concern itself with space; rather, it became something like the eye of a hurricane—that point of absolute stillness at the center of, and created by, the motion of the rushing winds.

A revealing episode having to do with flowers took place between Rikyū and Hideyoshi; it is an episode which symbolizes the dramatic tension between the two men. Hideyoshi, on hearing that the morning glories in Rikyū's private garden were in magnificent bloom, decided that he must see them and made an appointment to call on Rikyū one day. When he arrived, the morning glories had all been cut down; not a single one remained. Disgruntled, Hideyoshi entered the teahouse, where he found a single morning glory arranged in the *tokonoma*—a bloom of such perfection that it both satisfied and overwhelmed him.

Sukiya-zukuri: Reconciliation of Opposites

Just as the *nageire* style of flower arranging was perfected through its association with the quiet aesthetics of the tea ceremony, so *tatehana*, too, flourished as the style best suited to *shoin-zukuri*; Ikenobō Senkō (1575–1658), the second-generation master of the Ikenobō school of flower arrangement, achieved great success in integrating it into life at the Imperial Court.

As *nageire* took on sacred qualities through a process of gradual purification and refinement, *tatehana* underwent a reverse sort of transformation, gaining some of the freedom that *nageire* was discarding in its gradual narrowing of focus on a single, sacred flower. The two styles established their status as the Heaven (*ten*) and Earth (*chi*) of flower arrangement, which has now entered upon the age of Humanity (*hito*).

This new human style of arrangement is what we call by the name of ikebana today. Most Japanese associate the word "ikebana" with a plethora of schools and styles, but all of these modern developments came about only after the disparate worlds of *tatehana* and *nageire* had been established. All of them consist of different ways of fusing those two earlier styles—in such tremendous

Weeping willow in the "sand" style of flower arrangement (*suna no mono*), by Ikenobō Senkō. From *Ikenobō Senkō Rikka-zu*.

variety and independence that one could almost say each practitioner forms his own school nowadays.

In the realm of architecture, too, after Hideyoshi and Rikyū had perfected the distinctive *shoin* style and rustic teahouse style, a new style of residential architecture arose as a fusion of these two, called *sukiya-zukuri*.

This new style, which became the basis for modern residential architecture, is represented in the Katsura Detached Palace in Kyoto. Its fusion of the delicacy of the *sukiya* with the formality of *shoin-zukuri* proved extremely popular, and has even been praised as the essence of Japanese architecture.

The Japanese passion for flowers is woven from the sacredness of *tatehana* and the freedom of *nageire*. The resulting cloth of ikebana, with its hidden dramas of the heart of nature and of the human heart, has at last become truly a cloth of the people, one which each person can cut, style, dye, and wear freely as he or she pleases.

To arrange flowers is to express the life of flowers. Both of the traditional styles of flower arrangement expressed that life, each in its own way. Ancient Japanese did not look on the flower as an object and discern life within it; the flower itself was life, and for that reason they revered it as a god, felt close to it, believed in it, and extolled it.

At present, ikebana is thought of as a kind of plastic art using flowers as its medium. The arrangements shown in this book, however, do not represent that kind of ikebana, but rather the "ikebana of life"—based on my pursuit of and experience with the two basic strands of ikebana that have arisen out of the Japanese tradition of venerating flowers as divine.

Flower arranging in Japan has progressed from a temporary resting-place for Shinto gods to a ritual offering to Buddhist images, then on to an enjoyable leisure activity; from formal *tatehana* and spontaneous *nageire* to a wide variety of individual schools and styles. During all this change, what has been gained, and what lost? I am deeply struck by the tremendous number of things that have been lost over the years. And it strikes me that the true tradition to which we are heir is creativity itself.

The *shoin* of the Katsura Detached Palace, Kyoto.

Commentary on the Plates

1 MATERIAL: Pine
CONTAINER: Antique bronze vase, Muromachi period
(1333–1573)

All flower arrangement is a form of prayer. As I light the candles, stand the flowers, and give them water, I continually pray to something in nature. Through prayer, the starting point for all flower arrangement, the true heart of all plant life is revealed.

2 MATERIAL: Camellia
CONTAINER: Hanging boat-shaped bronze vase,
Momoyama period (1573–1615)

Year in and year out, the same radiant life blooms in flowers. A millennium ago, people gazed at the camellia with the same sense of wonder as we do today. Of course, each individual sees a different flower; yet, all can admire the ability of flowers to reflect the human heart. This led to the development of ikebana and to the perception that a single flower holds the whole universe within it.

3 MATERIAL: Two kinds of camellia
CONTAINER: Antique bronze vase, Edo period
(1615–1868)

Nothing gives me such a sense of a living soul as the sight of a towering tree. In a large camellia tree I see the vitality of a huge living thing built up over vast stretches of time. When I break off a branch and arrange it, I directly sense the souls of the ancient people who saw a god within such trees, and revered it. To arrange flowers is to become aware of the summit of heaven and the depths of the earth: to become aware, in short, of the universe.

4 MATERIAL: Japanese white pine, camellia,
moss-covered pine
CONTAINER: Antique bronze container,
Momoyama period (1573–1615)
LOCATION: Hōnen'in Temple, Kyoto

I was inspired to create this piece by the painting of a silver falcon on the sliding pine panel in the rear.

I arranged it so that the falcon would seem about to land on the trunk of the pine. For the trunk, I used an old, mossy pine branch; something forceful like this is necessary to balance off the falcon. For the pine needles, however, I used a Japanese white pine, which has great elegance and grace. This choice was determined by the painting of the falcon, which is so old that it is starting to peel off the wood. In combining flowers and other plants, this sort of attention to detail is vital if the composition is to come together as an integrated whole.

5 MATERIAL: Japanese apricot
CONTAINER: Antique bronze vase, Ming dynasty (1368–1644)
LOCATION: Hōnen'in Temple, Kyoto

Cherry blossoms are arranged when they are in full bloom, Japanese apricot blossoms when the buds become swollen and no more than a few have begun to bloom. This is because the cherry blossom represents the fullness of spring, with flowers everywhere, while the Japanese apricot is a harbinger, blooming when it is still cold to announce the coming of spring.

6 MATERIAL: Weeping willow, moss-covered pine, Japanese rohdea
CONTAINER: Antique bronze container, Momoyama period (1573–1615)
LOCATION: Hōnen'in Temple, Kyoto

The willow has long been revered in China and Japan for its spiritual qualities. In ikebana, it is used primarily from winter to early spring, almost never in the lushness of summer.

Because their branches are long and trailing, willows symbolize the hope that this world will endure and prosper. For this reason it is used chiefly at weddings and other celebratory events.

7 MATERIAL: Pink weeping Japanese apricot, moss-covered pine, white Japanese apricot, camellia
CONTAINER: Antique bronze container, Momoyama period (1573–1615)
LOCATION: Hōnen'in Temple, Kyoto

Ikebana is akin to music. The musical content of a composition determines whether it is to be a symphony or a sonata; similarly, the content of a flower arrangement determines its form. This composition is a floral symphony. Just as each part of a symphony has its own highlights, yet merges harmoniously with the others to form an integrated composition, so it is with the "sand" style of flower arrangement (*suna no mono*), seen here, as well as the "standing-flower" (*tatehana*) style.

8 MATERIAL: Weeping cherry
CONTAINER: Gold-leaf folding screen with bamboo backing, black lacquered candle stands
LOCATION: Hatakeyama Museum, Tokyo

The cherry blossom, a symbol of Japan, is a flower with particular meaning for Japanese people. The sight of cherry trees in full bloom brings a lump to my throat, conveying as it does the passionate longings and wishes of Japanese people since ancient times.

The variety of cherry used here is the weeping cherry, a particularly lovely variety. I arranged a pair of green bamboo stems behind a pair of gold screens, and arranged the cherries in a dynamic way, as if painting blossoms on the screen. Then I lit candles in the candle stands, making the arrangement perfect for nighttime blossom viewing.

9 MATERIAL: Wisteria, clematis, weeping cherry
CONTAINER: Black lacquered towel rack with *maki-e* design, Edo period (1615–1868), gold-leaf screen
LOCATION: Hatakeyama Museum, Tokyo

Once, when Picasso was painting flowers in a hothouse, the gardener who had raised them commented, "The beauty of flowers can't be conveyed in paintings, can it?" Picasso reportedly went home and looked at a Renoir painting of roses—and discovered that it was *more* beautiful than the real thing. The painting expressed the essence of beauty itself, which is more beautiful than any individual flower. Ikebana, too, uses natural objects to draw out the beauty at the heart of nature.

10 MATERIAL: Camellia, weeping cherry
CONTAINER: Red lacquered incense stand, Ch'ing dynasty (1644–1912), gold-leaf screen
LOCATION: Hatakeyama Museum, Tokyo

Because the camellia flower falls from its stem intact, in old times it was shunned by samurai, due to the

inauspicious association with beheading. Still, among ordinary Japanese the camellia has been well loved, and many varieties have originated in Japan.

Camellia leaves tend to collect dust, so it is important to clean them well before using the flowers in an arrangement. Water alone does not do a very good job, but if you wipe the leaves with a cloth soaked in alcohol, they will keep their glossy shine indefinitely. To keep the flower from falling off, a traditional technique that works very well is to use water that has stood awhile rather than freshly drawn water.

11 MATERIAL: Kerria, wisteria, clematis, black lily, *miyakowasure* (*Gymnaster savatieri*), fritillaria
CONTAINER: Gold-leaf folding screen, bamboo
LOCATION: Hatakeyama Museum, Tokyo

Like the cherry blossom arrangement in Fig. 8, this piece grew out of an idea I had for using screens. Attaching green bamboo directly to the screen would have damaged it, so I placed a stand behind the screen with a hook sticking out in front. Because green bamboo has a high water content, cut joints are apt to leak and create stains, so here I have used a waterproof sheet, cut to match the shape of the bamboo.

12 MATERIAL: (a) Osmund and Japanese butterbur, (b) Japanese apricot, (c) daffodil, (d) *miyakowasure* (*Gymnaster savatieri*), (e) fritillaria, (f) *kodemari* viburnum, (g) black lily
CONTAINER: Gold-painted clamshell

Springtime flowers have special sweetness and charm. To bring out the natural loveliness of these flowers, I arranged them each in a clamshell covered with gold-leaf, to look like a picture painted on gold. I enjoyed filling the shells with water and displaying them in this fashion on black lacquered trays.

13 MATERIAL: Jasmine, Japanese cymbidium
CONTAINER: White porcelain bowl, Momoyama period (1573–1615)

Being fond of wildflowers, I often use them in my arrangements. They do not absorb water well as a rule, however, unless I soak the cut stems in hot water for twenty seconds and then quickly stand them in deep cold water. To keep hot water from getting on the petals or leaves, I wrap them in newspaper and tilt the flower sideways when I immerse it. It is also vital to protect the flower from wind.

14 MATERIAL: Berries of berchemia racemosa vine
CONTAINER: Chinese silver cup, T'ang dynasty (A.D. 618–907)

The purpose of arranging flowers is to draw forth the true, inner beauty of nature. When we fall in love with someone, we endeavor to know that person's true mind or heart; in the same way, we must fall in love with flowers and plants if we hope to uncover their inmost heart. Finally, when we are able to perceive the heart of nature, we can no longer be satisfied with mere surface changes in shape, or shifts in coloration.

15 MATERIAL: Cherry blossom on charcoal
CONTAINER: Kiseto-ware flower container, Edo period (1615–1868)

This style of arrangement, called *sumibana*, or "charcoal flower," is a highly unusual, improvisational style. Charcoal was long the main fuel for heating in Japan. For *sumibana*, I wash the charcoal carefully, cut it to a convenient size, bore holes in it, and arrange flowers with the jet-black coal as a background. Charcoal has germ-killing properties, so the water stays clean and the flowers last a long time.

16 MATERIAL: Rose, wisteria, black lily, peony, fragrant snowbell
CONTAINER: Reproduction of a Chinese basket, Edo period (1615–1868)
LOCATION: Hatakeyama Museum, Tokyo

is something vibrant, with a strong sense of appropriateness. Beauty has order and balance and is never unnatural; it follows the great laws of the universe, and yet has perfect freedom.

No one can create beauty from a narrowly subjective perspective; rather, beauty results when a balance is reached between subjectivity and the principles of nature. Subjectivity alone is a poor guide in choosing combinations of flowers for ikebana. Only when one's subjective opinion harmonizes well with natural principles can it lead to vibrant beauty.

Beauty has the power to attract people everywhere; what most people in fact consider "beautiful," however,

17

MATERIAL: Two kinds of peony, dried wood
CONTAINER: Reproduction of a Chinese basket,
Edo period (1615–1868)
LOCATION: Hatakeyama Museum, Tokyo

When I obtained this peony, I sensed it whispering to me to do something gorgeous and showy with it. It seems to me that when we arrange flowers, they have already read our hearts and communicated something to us.

It is almost as if nature reads people's hearts and changes her expression accordingly. I think that art may be the means by which we come close to, and confirm, the human heart within nature.

18

MATERIAL: Wisteria, *Anemone flaccida*
CONTAINER: Metal Buddhist rice bowl, Kasuga table,
both Kamakura period (1185–1333)
LOCATION: Hatakeyama Museum, Tokyo

I love wisteria, but rather than the artificiality of vines on trellises, I vastly prefer the sight of wild wisteria wound around trees, blossoming high in the sky.

In the old capital of Nara, Kasuga Shrine, dedicated to the noble Fujiwara clan of ancient times, has taken the wisteria as its symbol for a simple reason: *Fuji* means "wisteria." I make a point of going there every

spring during the first half of May to see the wild wisteria flowering all around the shrine. It has such grace and dignity that it seems to recreate the elegance of the courtiers of old. Every year I stand there lost in admiration.

The hanging scroll shown here, which dates from the fourteenth century, portrays a famous poem, "*Kasuga kaishi*," composed at Kasuga Shrine; the table on which the arrangement stands, dating from the same period, is of a style unique to the shrine. I selected these objects relating to the shrine in token of my deep reverence for it.

19

MATERIAL: Japanese white pine, lily, wisteria, peony,
dead wood
CONTAINER: Antique bronze container, Momoyama
period (1573–1615)
LOCATION: Hatakeyama Museum, Tokyo

Wisteria is one of my favorite flowers, but it requires special effort to preserve it in cut form. I usually use saké as a preservative. You should cut the flower in the early morning or evening and immediately scrape off the outer surface of the cut end of the stem. Split the cut end and, while holding the flower upside down, pour as much saké into it as can be absorbed. Then place the flower in a deep vessel filled with a mixture of water and a small amount of saké, and let it rest for a few hours. Do not expose the flowers to the wind. This method is normally an effective way to keep the flowers looking fresh for a long time.

20

MATERIAL: Wisteria
CONTAINER: Glass vase

Many passages in Japanese classical literature express human feelings in terms of the beauty of nature. Unfortunately, art that attempts to reflect nature often lapses into unattractive mannerisms. When we attempt to recreate beauty, we must arrive at the point where no semblance of artifice or trickery is present. It is important to recognize the difference between something that is merely attractive, and true beauty.

21

MATERIAL: Scarlet *kazura* vine, violet
CONTAINER: Seventeenth-century Imari-ware vase

Beauty has many aspects, such as grace, sublimity, and pathos. Each of these qualities is determined not by form alone but, more importantly, by content. In the realm of ikebana, it is important to realize that while form is both a goal and a standard, it is also something that changes freely according to the content. There is no need to exaggerate the difficulty; all you need to do is grasp the nature of beauty intuitively, with your own eyes.

22

MATERIAL: Japanese iris
CONTAINER: Saké pitcher; Negoro lacquered wood,
Kamakura period (1185–1333)
LOCATION: Daichūji Temple, Shizuoka

Pared to the essentials, ikebana can be represented symbolically with points and lines, each with its own shading and dynamics. But flower arrangement is not just a matter of throwing these ingredients together any which way. Ample consideration must be given to the flow of the lines and to the exact placement of the points. Above all, only when everything is in tune with the dispensation of nature can the arrangement have the power to move people's hearts.

23

MATERIAL: Japanese iris
CONTAINER: Silver lacquered flower container in the form of a bridge (created by the author)
LOCATION: Daichūji Temple, Shizuoka

Surroundings of fresh green are refreshing and relaxing to the eyes and heart alike. One can only shake one's head in wonder at the powerful, mysterious attraction of nature.

I believe that ikebana must grasp the inner heart of this beauty of nature, with its great power to inspire, and infuse it with still greater beauty.

This composition is designed to show a maple tree in early leaf, with irises in bloom here and there. In ikebana, the iris is valued for its leaves, which are considered its focal point.

24

MATERIAL: Japanese iris
CONTAINER: Antique bronze container, Momoyama period (1573–1615)
LOCATION: Daichūji Temple, Shizuoka

In Kyoto, where I grew up, Ōta Shrine has long been famous for its irises, which grow in clusters. The iris is most beautiful not in strong sunlight on a fine day, but in the silence of dawn or dusk when there is a hint of rain in the air.

This work was inspired by the iris clusters at Ōta Shrine in Kyoto. I worked especially hard to achieve the sense of unity with the young maple leaves in the background, seen through the rattan blind.

25

MATERIAL: Japanese snow flower, Japanese hawthorn
CONTAINER: Korean white porcelain jar, Li dynasty, eighteenth century, folding screen by Kanzan Shimomura (1873–1930)

Every plant has its own color, shape, and other fundamental characteristics. We may want to select flowers with similar characteristics for an arrangement, or those with differing ones. In the art of ikebana, either approach is acceptable. Only the accumulation of experience can teach us the way that is more appropriate for a specific occasion.

For this work, I wanted to retain the sense of peacefulness generated by the silver gilding on the screen. Accordingly, I selected flowers with compatible colors and characteristics that would harmonize with those of the screen.

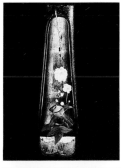

26

MATERIAL: Japanese peach blossom, peony
CONTAINER: Mother-of-pearl-inlaid vase

times and in all places. In ikebana, they are used to complement one another.

In Japan we speak of "stillness in motion" and "motion in stillness," and place great value on the ability to discover each attribute within its opposite: silence lurking in what appears to be violent motion; passion and movement welling out of what appears to be utter stillness . . . Perhaps most works of ikebana express the latter.

This composition expresses "motion in stillness" through the use of faintly pink peach buds and peony buds.

All things contain elements of motion and stillness. These opposing attributes are always present, at all

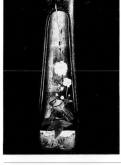

27

MATERIAL: Peach branch and fruit
CONTAINER: Antique gourd vase, Momoyama period (1573–1615)

tainers. Originally, the vessels were the prime focus of attention, not the flowers. That explains why, in Japan, flower containers have never been looked down on as mere tools for the display of flowers.

Match the container to the flowers, and the flowers to the container—this is a primary rule of flower arrangement.

The gourd I used here is some four centuries old, but it merges beautifully with the eroticism of the peaches, each complementing the other. Such perfect union and harmony between the container and the contained is wonderfully refreshing.

Proper appreciation of ikebana requires that attention be paid not only to the flowers but also to their con-

28

MATERIAL: Japanese pampas grass, Saint-John's-wort
CONTAINER: Antique basket, Edo period (1615–1868)

too easy to rely solely on the size of the arrangement and the abundance of flowers, making the effect rather monotonous. Each fleeting expression of the flowers must be caught, and their diversity portrayed, if the arrangement is to bring out their full charm.

I try to focus on and enhance the full diversity of expressions worn by flowers in their natural environments: clusters of blossoms, flowers arrayed in a luxuriant mass, and the lonely elegance of a solitary bloom. The basket here, which is some three hundred years old, was designed to be worn on the back while gathering edible wild plants.

Nothing fills the human heart like the sight of a wealth of flowers arranged in a large pot or basket. But it is all

29 MATERIAL: Morning glory
CONTAINER: Bush-clover single-panel screen
LOCATION: Daichūji Temple, Shizuoka

To use morning glories in an arrangement, you must gather them the previous evening, cutting buds that appear likely to bloom the next morning. Unwind the vine, insert the cutting in deep water in a fairly tall con-tainer, and place it outside where it will be protected from wind and can turn toward the sun. The next morning, the buds will burst into bloom and the tendrils will have turned up, not down, making them much easier to work with. Morning-glory petals tend to come off easily, and not all of the buds will bloom, so you should prepare more than you anticipate using. The trick to using morning glories is to get the buds to open properly. In this composition, I have portrayed a cluster of morning glories blooming on a single screen; I put peat moss at the base of the plants to keep them moist.

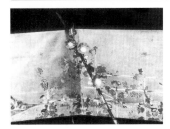

30 MATERIAL: Morning glory
CONTAINER: Bamboo, gold-leaf folding screen with *rimpa* design, Edo period (1615–1868)
LOCATION: Daichūji Temple, Shizuoka

The sight of a rough bamboo fence covered with morning glories is one of the traditional pleasures of a Japanese summer. This screen dates from the early seventeenth century; the moment I first saw it I fell in love with it and purchased it. I planned from the start to have real morning glories bloom around it someday, but years went by without my ever coming upon the perfect morning glories. This arrangement is, for me, a dream come true.

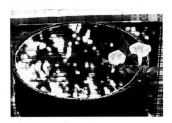

31 MATERIAL: Morning glory
CONTAINER: Iron flower container, Meiji period (1868–1912)
LOCATION: Daichūji Temple, Shizuoka

Without water, cut flowers wither and die. Water is life itself. Here, I have made water the focal point of the arrangement, with morning glories like the spirit of water. There is an old saying that the condition of water reflects the condition of the heart; I kept that in mind while creating this composition.

32 MATERIAL: *Yūgao (Lagenaria siceraria)*
CONTAINER: Antique iron stirrup, Edo period (1615–1868)
LOCATION: Daichūji Temple, Shizuoka

Whenever I use wildflowers in a tearoom, I always cover them with dewlike beads of water, first on the backs of the petals and leaves, then carefully on the front. Water has the effect of infusing life into flowers.

Flowers for the tea ceremony, however lovely, do not deserve a second glance if they have not been sprinkled with water. The arranger must select the moment when the flower is most beautiful, then sprinkle it with water. Seeing a flower glow with life is the pleasure and purpose of flowers for the tea ceremony.

33 MATERIAL: Morning glory
CONTAINER: Old bamboo
LOCATION: Daichūji Temple, Shizuoka

A single flower has its own not-to-be-denied heart, which it expresses in a straightforward way. If I hesitate, it loses vitality, so I do the arrangement in one burst of inspiration.

34 MATERIAL: Oyama magnolia, mountain hydrangea
CONTAINER: Bronze hanging oil lamp, Momoyama period (1573–1615)
LOCATION: Hatakeyama Museum, Tokyo

Suspended or hanging flowers should have a feeling of lightness. The sensation of hanging in midair is often likened to the light and airy sensation of riding in a ship; the use of too many flowers creates a heavy effect, which spoils this mood. The painting is by Kanō Tanyū (1602–74).

35
MATERIAL: Dead pine, Japanese ivy
CONTAINER: Saké pitcher; black Negoro lacquered wood, Muromachi period (1333–1573)
LOCATION: Hatakeyama Museum, Tokyo

The very word "ikebana" is derived from the Japanese word for life, and it is essential that the materials used in an arrangement be alive. When I use an old piece of dead wood such as that shown here, I must do it in such a way that life courses through it. This wood is something I brought back with me from the slopes of Mt. Fuji; the vines entwined around it bring it to life.

36
MATERIAL: Lily, wild summer plants
CONTAINER: Bamboo basket
LOCATION: Kawase residence, Nara

When I have guests, I often place garden flowers in a bamboo basket and leave it casually at the entrance. The flowers express my welcome to my guests. It is important that the flowers be as fresh as possible, as if just plucked from the garden or a hill in back of one's home, and that they be well sprinkled with water to emphasize the beauty of the moment.

37
MATERIAL: Berry of *fusasuguri* (*Ribes rubrum*), wild strawberry
CONTAINER: Wooden lacquer pail, Momoyama period (1573–1615)
LOCATION: Kawase residence, Nara

This vessel is a lacquer pail, used to gather the sap from Japanese sumac trees, from which lacquer is made. It was originally a practical, functional item, but true beauty often arises out of utility. In ikebana, it is important to have the eyes to discover beautiful containers for flowers.

38
MATERIAL: Japanese spirea, bellflower (*Campanula punctata*), wisteria vine
CONTAINER: Antique bamboo hanging basket, Edo period (1615–1868), wooden pole, Tempyō period (A.D. 710–794)
LOCATION: Kawase residence, Nara

The board from which this basket is hanging, called a *suibachi*, is designed so that one can enjoy hanging flowers anywhere. These boards come in a wide variety of shapes, but they are all of simple construction (consisting simply of a hook nailed into a board), and can be easily made.

The *suibachi* shown here is made from wood used in a temple a thousand years ago. In selecting the flower, I took special pains to find something that would not spoil the dignity of this antique wood.

39
MATERIAL: Japanese pampas grass, clematis, two kinds of lily, *kawaranadeshiko* (*Dianthus superbus*)
CONTAINER: Reproduction of a Chinese bamboo basket, Edo period (1615–1868)
LOCATION: Kawase residence, Nara

Flowers are loved for their colors, but it is also good to appreciate them in silhouette, as shown here. The colors of the garden in the background support the silhouetted ikebana. Flowers used in this way must have graceful lines.

40
MATERIAL: Japanese stewartia
CONTAINER: Iron hanging oil lamp, Momoyama period (1573–1615)
LOCATION: Kawase residence, Nara

Traditional Japanese houses have special places to appreciate ikebana—stages for the art, if you will. Like performers in the spotlight, flowers placed there take on a vivid glow.

41 MATERIAL: *Adenophora triphylla*, speedwell, a variety of superb pink
CONTAINER: Water pitcher; Negoro lacquered wood, Muromachi period (1333–1573)
LOCATION: Kawase residence, Nara

This photograph, and the five preceding, were all taken at the home of a friend in Nara. It is an old farmhouse, well suited to the atmosphere of the ancient capital, with many thousand-year-old timbers. Everything about the place, from the building to the furnishings and garden, is in the finest and most refined Japanese tradition.

In such a home, ikebana that is too artfully designed stands out oddly, unsuited to the general atmosphere and disturbing to the overall harmony. The type of flower used also must not detract from the dignity of the surroundings. For this occasion I used flowers and grasses from the garden and from nearby hills and fields. Flowers have no existence apart from their natural climate; flowers nurtured in the local climate are always the most beautiful.

42 MATERIAL: Lotus
CONTAINER: Flower basin, gold-leaf folding screen, Edo period (1615–1868)
LOCATION: Yoshida residence, Kyoto

When using marsh flowers, great pains must be taken to ensure that they absorb an adequate amount of water. Otherwise, even if the flowers themselves last, the leaves will fade and wither before your eyes.

For lotus flowers and similar plants such as water lilies, a special pump must be used. If you don't have such a pump, turn the end of a plant-mister upside down and insert it in the end of the lotus stem as if giving an injection. Pour water into the entire stem until it is stiff and turgid. A special pump for ikebana does the job simply and speedily.

This composition recreates the sight of a lotus pond indoors. I used several basins with *kenzan* for the flowers.

43 MATERIAL: Lotus
CONTAINER: Antique bronze container, Edo period (1615–1868)
LOCATION: Daichūji Temple, Shizuoka

The pleasure of arranging flowers lies in discovering the beauty of form, which gradually becomes apparent through the process of simplifying the materials used. By cutting a flower, you are able to penetrate the reality of its form—a reality hidden while it is blooming in its natural state. This is the unique fascination of ikebana; if not for that, it would be a sin to cut the flowers. With this composition, too, the process of cutting and arranging these lotus blossoms taught me things about the heart of the lotus I had never known before.

44 MATERIAL: Lotus
CONTAINER: Antique bronze container
LOCATION: Daichūji Temple, Shizuoka

I believe that while nature is perfect, human beings are essentially imperfect. I believe that that is why human beings are drawn to the perfection of nature, and seek it out. Unable to achieve perfection, we are condemned to go on searching for it forever. This constant hope is what it means to be alive, and what forms the wellspring of creation.

I made this composition with the legendary Chinese beauty Yang Kuei-fei in mind. (Something about the red lotus suggests Chinese beauty to me.) After finishing the arrangement, I gazed at it tirelessly for a long time, as if seeing a vision of the exquisite Yang Kuei-fei enshrined behind bamboo blinds.

45 MATERIAL: Lotus leaves, red balloon flower, rose of Sharon, *sagiso* (*Pecteilis radiate*)
CONTAINER: Antique bronze container, Muromachi period (1333–1573)
LOCATION: Daichūji Temple, Shizuoka

Certain precautions must be taken when using copper vessels. Always hold the vessel in a soft cloth: Do not take it in your bare hands, as copper does not react favorably to skin oil, fingerprints, or salt. Before putting it away, wipe it carefully with a cloth that has been soaked in warm water and well wrung out; then set it facedown on a dry towel, out of the sun, and let it air for a couple of days. Otherwise, the vessel will develop unremovable stains.

46 MATERIAL: Japanese maple, lily
CONTAINER: Bamboo basket
LOCATION: Daichūji Temple, Shizuoka

Here I have used outdoor scenery as a background for ikebana. Unless you are careful in attempting this, the arrangement will simply blend into the outdoor scenery and lose its impact. If you supply something to function like the frame of a painting, as I have done with the bamboo blind here, the arrangement will stand out.

47   MATERIAL: *Karukaya* (*Themeda japonica*), clematis vine
CONTAINER: Bamboo flower stand (created by the author)

I love lonely gardens overgrown with grass-like deserted ruins. Standing alone in such a garden makes me feel like some solitary figure, nostalgic for another, more prosperous time and feeling a sense of eternity and the transitory nature of human existence.

I tried in this work to express an image of such a deserted garden in summertime, complete with its overgrowth of grass. I hope that the disheveled clump of meadow grass and the few remaining fragments of flowers of the wind-weathered clematis convey my feelings.

48   MATERIAL: Clematis, Japanese pampas grass, hydrangea
CONTAINER: Silver lacquered flower container (created by the author)

One of the principal charms of ikebana is the charm of line. Even a very few flowers can give an impression of great size because they dominate space with their lines. If I can reproduce the essential, compelling lines of nature in my work, I can ask for nothing more.

49   MATERIAL: Clematis
CONTAINER: Black lacquered hanging flower container (created by the author)

I arranged clematis in this hanging flower container, which I designed myself so that both sides appear to be the front. The secret to using a container like this is not to arrange the two sides in the same way, but to make them complement and enrich each other. If one side shows an opened flower, for example, the other should feature folded buds. The two sides are bound together by bringing vines skillfully into play.

50   MATERIAL: Balloon flower, plum fruits, Japanese bulrush
CONTAINER: Japanese paper

Origami, the art of folding paper in various designs, is like ikebana: an ancient art transmitting the soul of Japan. In this work, I used folded paper as the container for a hanging arrangement. I put a small holder behind the paper to secure it, punched holes in the paper, and inserted the flowers through them. The flowers need to be arranged in a clean, crisp way or they will not harmonize with the lines of the origami.

51   MATERIAL: *Left:* Clematis, *miyakowasure* (*Gymnaster savatieri*), bush clover; *center:* stachyurus, lily; *right:* kerria, lily of the valley, *chōjisō* (*Amesonia elliptica*)
CONTAINER: Bamboo basket, glass screen (created by author)

Kakebana, or hanging flowers, is an easy way for anyone to enjoy arranging flowers. Traditional Japanese houses have a *tokonoma*, or alcove, with a hook in the front for displays of hanging flowers, but modern houses tend to lack such a space. To compensate for this, I created a glass screen with hooks for hanging flowers. When hanging more than one arrangement, take care to space them carefully to avoid a monotonous effect.

52   MATERIAL: Superb pink, balloon flower, *karukaya* (*Themeda japonica*), wild morning-glory leaves
CONTAINER: Antique bird cage, Edo period (1615–1868)

The moment I saw this bird cage, I envisioned it filled with a profusion of fall flowers.

Whenever flowers are to be viewed through a screen of some sort, there should be three times as many flowers as actually meet the eye, to avoid a skimpy effect. To suggest depth, arrange the flowers layer upon layer. Finally, it is most effective if you skillfully mix arrangements of masses of flowers with places where a single flower is highlighted.

53 MATERIAL: Superb pink, Japanese pampas grass
CONTAINER: Crescent-shaped vase of lacquered silver
(created by the author)

In Japan, the moon is an important motif in design. I myself love the crescent moon far more than the full moon, and designed this flower holder accordingly. I went to some trouble specifying just how I wanted to bring out both the roundness of the moon and the two points. Finally, I covered it with silver lacquer.

To avoid canceling out the delicate lines of the crescent moon, I used a super-fine variety of eulalia, accented by a single superb pink.

54 MATERIAL: Balloon flower, striped reed
CONTAINER: Kneading trough, Edo period (1615–1868)

The urge to arrange flowers arises out of an overlapping and heightening of two opposite urges: the impulse to resist nature and the impulse to merge with it. In this work I have portrayed a photographic impression of a profusion of Chinese bellflowers, but it is the strong presence of the stone that makes the arrangement succeed.

55 MATERIAL: Bush clover
CONTAINER: Iron hanging oil lamp, Edo period
(1615–1868)
LOCATION: Daichūji Temple, Shizuoka

Hagi, or Japanese bush clover, does not produce a flashy flower, but the sight of a profusion of *hagi* blossoms has a certain coquetry and enchantment all its own. I have no difficulty understanding why the ancient Japanese loved this fall flower above all others.

56 MATERIAL: Japanese pampas grass, superb pink,
yūgao (*Lagenaria siceraria*), wild autumn plants
CONTAINER: Antique bamboo basket, Edo period
(1615–1868)

When combining a large number of different grasses and flowers, you must sort out the leaves properly, or they will not produce a beautiful harmony.

In this piece I was careful to use the leaves of all these autumn flowers to good effect. In order to integrate the composition with the container, I put a base holding water under the basket.

57 MATERIAL: Six-leaved akebia (*Stauntonia hexaphylla*)
CONTAINER: Antique bamboo basket, Edo period
(1615–1868)

I made this composition out of love for the fruit of the *mube* (*Stauntonia hexaphylla*). The fruit is heavy and needs to be entwined with something else for stability. Here I used a single variety of *mube*, weaving it through the interstices of the basket and tipping the basket over sideways to emphasize the heaviness of the fruit.

58 MATERIAL: Persimmon branches and fruit, chrysanthemum, Japanese ivy
CONTAINER: Wooden and bamboo folding screen
LOCATION: Gotō Art Museum, Tokyo

I wanted to express a very clear sense of late autumn in this scene set against a kind of folding-screen flower frame. In my mind, autumn is to plants as old age is to human beings.

The linear features of this arrangement are an important factor in communicating a sense of the all-encompassing fulfillment that wonderfully characterizes old age, and that the young sprouts and flowers of early spring lack.

This piece combines a number of conflicting elements that react together—strong and weak, large and small, heavy and light, hard and soft—arriving at a climactic interrelationship.

The solitary leaf clinging to the tip of a branch, projecting a complex image of the emotions borne by the aged, colorfully relates to the feelings of late autumn.

I carefully chose additional leaves that were withered, discolored, and worm-eaten.

59

MATERIAL: Foxtail, millet
CONTAINER: Antique wooden water pail, Edo period (1615–1868)
LOCATION: Gotō Art Museum, Tokyo

Ikebana must express a sense of the seasons. This work is an expression of thanks for the rich harvest of autumn.

60

MATERIAL: Wild five-leaved akebia, assorted vegetables and fruit
CONTAINER: Antique bamboo basket, Edo period (1615–1868)
LOCATION: Gotō Art Museum, Tokyo

Drawn by the beauty of a vine with akebia fruit attached, I combined it with a variety of edible autumn fruits. When using a utilitarian basket as a flower holder, I tip the basket up a little in back to make it appear lighter.

61

MATERIAL: Chrysanthemum, aster
CONTAINER: Antique bamboo basket
LOCATION: Gotō Art Museum, Tokyo

There is a certain trick to arranging chrysanthemums. They do not react well to metal, so you must never cut them with scissors, but always snap the stems with your hands. The chrysanthemum flower is long-last-

ing, but the leaves tend to wither quickly, so two or three hours before starting the arrangement, you should take the following steps.

First, hold the chrysanthemum upside down under a water faucet and pour water on the base of the stem and the backs of the leaves. Then, still holding it upside down, wrap it in newspaper, plunge the stem in a deep, water-filled container, and break off the base of the stem with your hands, underwater. If you leave it that way for several hours, it will absorb water well. When a chrysanthemum has started to wilt, treat it in the same way and it will revive surprisingly.

62

MATERIAL: Chrysanthemum
CONTAINER: Bamboo flower stand
LOCATION: Gotō Art Museum, Tokyo

As anyone can see from the arrangements in this book, I frequently use fresh bamboo in my works. No special effort is required to preserve bamboo stalks without leaves; however, to preserve the leaves, it is necessary to take special measures.

Bamboo leaves grow from the stem joints. First, trim away all unneeded leaves. Next take some kind of

metal spike and pierce the joints through from the top of the stem down to the joint where the leaves are growing. Then fill the space with boiling salt water poured in from the top, and cap the end with crumpled newspaper or something of that sort. Leave overnight.

The next day, after confirming that the leaves are absorbing water without difficulty, drain the salt water and replace with fresh water at room temperature. Continue to replenish the water whenever the level falls. If you use this method, the bamboo should last about a month. Otherwise the leaves will curl up within an hour.

63

MATERIAL: Japanese maple, weeping willow
CONTAINER: Bamboo vase (created by the author)

The common Japanese term for flower arranging is ikebana, as the common name for the tea ceremony is *chanoyu*. However, each art also has other names—*Kadō* (the Way of Flowers) and *Sadō* (the Way of Tea)—that refer more to the philosophy behind them than to the

techniques involved. *Dō* in Japanese means a path or a way. Its use here signifies that the purpose of an art is not simply to acquire the necessary skills but, rather, that the art exists in itself as a spiritual goal in life as well as the way to achieve that goal. *Dō*, in this sense, represents both universal truth and the process of attaining truth.

I realize that it may seem contradictory to refer to a goal and the process of achieving the goal in identical terms. But I consider that the process of flower arrangement embodies a universal truth at every moment; when I am arranging flowers, I can sense eternity.

64

MATERIAL: Japanese maple, aster (Michaelmas daisy)
LOCATION: Daihōin, Kyoto

Whenever I arrange autumn leaves, my nerves are always on edge. Autumn leaves are extremely vulnerable to wind and dryness, so generally they don't last long. After I cut a branch, I sprinkle it all over with an aqueous solution of menedael, wrap it—leaves and all—in plastic or some such thing, and put it back in the aqueous solution. That way I find the leaves last a fairly long time.

65 MATERIAL: Japanese maple

Ikebana is basically an indoor art, but on occasion it makes a refreshing change to set an arrangement outdoors. Here I used the river as container; the sight of autumn leaves scattered on the surface of a river has long been part of the Japanese image of fall, and many *waka* (traditional short poems) have been composed on that theme. Here I sought to contrast the leaves under the water with those on top.

66 MATERIAL: Chrysanthemum, dried bamboo
CONTAINER: Bamboo basket, Edo period (1615–1868)
LOCATION: Daihōin, Kyoto

As soon as I finished this arrangement, the chrysanthemums were bathed in a sublime light, as if they had mysteriously summoned it. The sight of the chrysanthemum arrangement wrapped in the glow of an autumn sunset was so noble and awe-inspiring that everyone present fell silent, as if we were gazing at the very spirit of flowers. No one stirred until the light had faded and gone.

67 Autumn flower party in Kyoto

One autumn day when the leaves were beautiful, I held a flower party at a temple in Kyoto with some

close friends, on the theme of autumn leaves. A flower party is a traditional Japanese gathering at which people, nature, and history are united in perfect harmony. Everyone wore a kimono woven with a pattern of autumn flowers, and dined together while looking out at the leaves in the garden. This was followed by tea; then everyone present composed a poem and made a flower arrangement to express the heart of that poem. The magnificent drama between nature and human beings that unfolded that day, from early morning until evening, left me feeling that I myself had become one with the autumn leaves.

68 MATERIAL: Pine (live and dead branches), Japanese maple
CONTAINER: Antique bronze vase, Momoyama period (1573–1615)
LOCATION: Daihōin, Kyoto

The ideal behind the *tatehana* ("standing-flower") style is to have what is being presented in a vase evoke an entire mountain panorama. When you walk up a mountain, you see a variety of natural manifestations: huge trees that look as though they could stir the sky, valleys, waterfalls and streams, etc. Similarly, you sense the kaleidoscopic variations of nature among the elements of a *tatehana* arrangement.

This work suggests the scenery of a mountain covered with leaves changing their hues in autumn.

69 MATERIAL: Artificial chrysanthemum
CONTAINER: *Hira kusudama*

The white chrysanthemum symbolizes Japan's Imperial household. This composition is a special form of interior decoration for the Imperial Palace (known as *hira kusudama*), of my own design. I tried to express the spirit of the Imperial family through the purity and dignity of the white chrysanthemum. It is hanging against an early-seventeenth-century *fusuma-e* (sliding panel consisting of painted paper stretched over a light wooden frame).

70 MATERIAL: Japanese maple, hanging scroll by Kanō Motonobu (1476–1554)

Gentle beams of autumn sunshine came pouring through the latticed window of the teahouse. Outside, autumn leaves were drinking in the sunshine, radiant in all their glory. I felt for a moment as if a branch of those bright leaves had entered the teahouse along with the sun. Immediately, I went out and broke off a leafy branch, wrapped damp moss around the end, and stuck it in the latticed window. Something still seemed lacking, so I added a monochrome ink painting of deer at play in an autumn field.

71

MATERIAL: Trichosanthes, aster (Michaelmas daisy)
CONTAINER: Seto-ware vase, Kamakura period
(1185–1333)
LOCATION: Mizutani residence, Kyoto

I arrange late autumn flowers the way they might be expected to look in their natural state. The plants of that season are likely to be damaged or withered, besides being flowerless. It is the time when everything seems to be quietly receding and preparing for a winter of dormancy.

I prefer to select an imperfect vase, one with some flaw or a coarse texture, to harmonize with my late autumnal arrangements.

To arrange flowers under such circumstances is the supreme challenge.

72

MATERIAL: Dried lotus
CONTAINER: Seto-ware vase, Kamakura period
(1185–1333)
LOCATION: Hatakeyama Museum, Tokyo

As winter approaches, leaves fall and grasses wither, heralding the start of a lull in their life cycle. The act of arranging winter plants arises from wonder at the power hidden within them.

Ikebana is more than just shaping materials into a pleasing form. The inspiration to arrange flowers arises only when we touch upon the mystery of the vital force found within the subtle changes plants undergo. That is why the same flower can seem to wear a thousand different expressions.

73

MATERIAL: Dried lotus
CONTAINER: Broken vase by Shirō Tsujimura

Everyone thinks flowers are beautiful. Yet, among flowers, there are wretched ones, arrogant ones, shamelessly wanton ones. When the essential spirit of all those flowers is brought out, however, it becomes Beauty. That's what ikebana is.

74

MATERIAL: Camellia

Flowers, to me, are aspiration, and life itself.

I sense that even as I am looking at flowers, the flowers are looking back at me.

About the Author

Toshirō Kawase was born in Kyoto in 1948, the youngest son in a family of prominent florists (for generations their shop, Hana-ichi, has been the official purveyor of flower arrangement materials to Kyoto's famous Ikenobō School of Ikebana). From an early age Kawase took a great interest in flowers, creating his first arrangements instinctively, without formal instruction. By the time he was ten he was creating flower arrangements before groups in private homes.

One day, while delivering fresh flowers from his family's store to the Buddhist temple where the Ikenobō School had its headquarters, young Kawase saw the aged teacher of the school's master bowed in prayer. From that moment Kawase became convinced that, in his words, the spirit of flower arrangement must be like "the spirit of a prayer—*inori*."

After finishing high school in Kyoto, Kawase went to Tokyo to study drama. In 1970 he studied theatrical production at the University of Paris, but after two and a half years in Europe he once again felt drawn to the world of flowers, and returned to Japan.

Back in Kyoto, Kawase joined the Ikenobō Cultural Academy and took as his teacher for life Master Kōzō Okada. He still remembers that at his very first lesson, he was inspired by Master Okada's *tatehana* ("standing flower") style of flower arranging, which was very different from the traditional form at Ikenobō. He renewed his quest for mastery of the art of ikebana, attempting to combine the principle of *inori* with the style of *tatehana*. Then, in the mid-1970's, he became acquainted with Hisao Kanze's Nō performances, which inspired Kawase with the image of "a flower at prayer." Finally he realized that the only way he could realize his vision of flowers was by creating a new form of flower arrangement that transcended the principles of any one school of ikebana.

In 1976, after the death of his mother, Kawase once again moved to Tokyo. Then came an unexpected and dramatic encounter. While on a part-time assignment arranging flowers at a restaurant in Tokyo's fashionable Harajuku district, Kawase met the world-famous fashion designer Issey Miyake. Miyake was struck by the originality of his creations and introduced Kawase to other notable figures of Japan's contemporary art and design world. Since then Kawase has taught his style and techniques of ikebana to thousands throughout Japan. Unlike the typical master of a traditional art in Japan, however, he has not taken on any disciples; he has no wish to establish certain set principles of flower arranging, but rather to encourage a love for the art of flowers in everyday life. Kawase feels that by teaching his own vision of flower arranging, he will be able to inspire a love of the essence of Japanese ikebana that everyone can share. As a flower artist without a school, Kawase takes as his challenge the expression of flower arranging not as a hobby or diversion but as a metaphor for the Japanese mind and culture.